Let Go of the Load
Sonja P. Davis

Copyright © 2019 Sonja P. Davis

All rights reserved. No part of this book may be reproduced or transmitted in any form or by any means, electronic or mechanical, including photocopying, recording or by any information storage and retrieval system, without permission in writing from the publisher.

Divine Encounter Publishing—Louisville, KY
ISBN: 978-1-7332146-0-5
Library of Congress Control Number: 2019909412
Let Go of the Load | Sonja P. Davis
Available Formats: eBook | Paperback distribution

Dedication

The perfect creation of God. A spiritual being with a soul, living in a body.

To anyone who's disabled, overwhelmed, distraught, brokenhearted, abused, and abandoned. Get your fight back. Choose Jesus. Go the 12 rounds with Him. Undoubtedly, you got the victory.

To anyone that needs to be restored, and feeling all hope is gone. Keep the faith. Keep believing. Keep trusting, because we serve a God that can do anything but fail. Choose to focus on God and not your problems, no matter what is going on in your life. Keep standing on the Promises of God. He is behind the scenes working things out for your good.

"Get Hope Restored"
"Receive indescribable Peace."
"Have unspeakable and sustaining Joy."

#TroubleInYourWay
FaithWorks
#JesusWillFixIt
#BelieveAndSurelyReceive
#PeaceAndDeliverance

Contents

Dedication iii
Acknowledgments vii
Introduction ix
Poetry: Times Up Rise UP / Me Too 1
Understanding Life's Trials 12
Hidden Figures 21
It's Just Like That 24
Judging & Repentance 27
Bitterness 29
Depression 39
Addiction 41
Post-traumatic Stress Disorder (PTSD) 49
Alzheimer's & Dementia 52
Be Encouraged 59
Let's Go to Church 69
Song of Praise (Running to You) 74
My Walk with God 77
Conclusion 83
About the Author 89

Acknowledgments

First and foremost, I have to thank God for showing me just how mighty and powerful He is. And for allowing me to "Let Go of the Load," which is a vessel of love to bless His people.

This book would not have been possible without the expertise, professionalism, and support from Erica Hughes and the team at New Book Authors. You are assisting me in telling my story and its glorifying God worldwide. Thank you for your patience and for demonstrating excellent customer service. Your follow-up is outstanding, which makes you a great organization. I am so grateful. And you should be rewarded for it.

Thank you, and I love you, everyone who has blessed, supported, cared, and prayed for me through this journey, I see you. My heart is full of adoration towards all of you. My husband Charlie, my daughter RayRay, and my son Ronnie. My grandchildren, JaCarie, Kaivon, Kyeli, and Kayla. My brothers, Pierre and Carlos. My Goddaughters, Natosha, Falesha, LaQuesha, and Shaneka. My mother-n-law, Laura Bates, sister-n-law Dawn White, and my beautiful Aunt Elnora.

God has blessed me with some beautiful Angels, amazing Soul Sistahs, and some outstanding Prayer Warriors. I am extremely grateful to have you all in my life. Thank you, and I love you from the bottom of my heart. Tonie Courtney, Wendy Goodwin, Ann Johnson, Norma Jean Preston, Sonnie Judkins, Zoe Commings, Montilla Seewright, Bonita Williams, Debra Rowe, Sheila Bivens, Angie Ross, Tianda Johnson, and the KSU Family. Dorissa Hobbs, Elease Tilford, Paula Thornton, Marvina Marshall, Diane Thornton, Faye Leavell, Patricia Williams, Sherryll Summers, Helen Swain, Janet Stroud, Juanita Granady, Deborah Strong, Jenyl Johnson, Jennie Hewitt, Donna DeJesus, Emma Edwards, Rev. Laurice Martin, Monica Graham, Aunt Sylvia, and Syl's Lounge, Internal & External Girlfriends from Humana Inc. Lace Social Club Members, The Bunco Bunnies, Diamond and Pearl Divas Red Hat Society, Bates Memorial Baptist Church Family, Pastor Carl E. Garmon, Sr. and the Prayer Line Ministry Family.

Introduction

In the face of adversity, I want to be an inspiration because I have the gracious hand of God on my life, and I'm well able to fulfill my destiny. Besides, if truth be told, "I'm just a nobody trying to tell everybody about somebody who can save anybody." (The Williams Brothers).

In the Horse Racing world, I'm a "Longshot", so don't count me out, include me in your exotic bets, in my heart I believe, I am able to do this, because I've been set apart for a specific purpose, and God has predetermined it, that I was going to win.

It was in 2009, where I went from cheering and given out high-fives, to wailing and receiving deepest sympathies to worship. The same year when a Longshot "Mine That Bird" won the Kentucky Derby, the same year my Daddy died. Also, the same year my marriage had reached its breaking point, and the same year the "King of Pop" Michael Jackson died.

As I let go of my heavy load and release the pain within, I recall the times when my parents were excited about celebrating the Kentucky Derby. They would spend all kinds of money preparing for this big day. We would get up early Derby morning setting up and preparing for guests to arrive. Mama would be in the backroom, entertaining with guests that stayed the weekend with them. My brother, my Dad, and I would go outside, ensuring that the tent is up in the backyard. Two car garage turns into a nightclub. Deck furniture is out. Bar stocked with Topshelf liquor. And to make certain we have the ingredients for "Mint Julep" (KY derby signature drink), also waiting for the 75in screen TV with a massive surround system is delivered and setup. All this was for their guests to enjoy themselves throughout the day, leading up to the big Kentucky Derby race "The Run for the Roses." This race hosted annually at Churchill Downs in Louisville, Kentucky on the first Saturday in May.

Afterward, my parents and I would go into the kitchen to prepare for this marvelous Derby breakfast. It consists of, "Bacon, Sausage, Scrambled Eggs, Creamy Slow Cooked Grits, Fried Potatoes & Onions, Hungry Jack Biscuits, Fried Apples, and a Rabbit fried smelling like Chicken, then smothered in Brown Gravy, including, Coffee and Orange Juice. Oh, do not let me forget about drinking Grapefruit Juice. It supposed to burn up all the fat we just ate. We would be laughing out loud. I know this was a bit much, but this preparation was our process preparing to study, which improved our chances of winning before placing our bets, some may say, "making a wager."

After that hearty breakfast, it was time to move to the living room to focus on the big race. Along with pen and paper at hand, we would have a racing form (booklet containing information about a horse), the sports section of the Courier-Journal newspaper, and a scratch sheet (shows horses withdrawn from a race, and statistics for the horses running) before placing our bets. We wanted to know what the weatherman predictions were during the race because it always played a role in placing our bets. If the weather forecast rain, we would look for a horse that runs well on a muddy track. We checked past performances, the wins and losses, the speed, its class, the odds, and the Contenders (horse's competition). We also wanted to know the owner, trainer, and which horse, being my Dad's favorite jockeys, were riding. More importantly, the parent of the horse; the "Sire" (horse's father) can have an impact on a horse...does he have genes like a Champion? As a result, we have our top three "destined to win.

After all, my Dad would always add in a 4th horse, a "Longshot." It may be one with the longest odds, unlikely to win, but based on key races previously won, got him to qualify to race in the

Kentucky Derby. His chances are just as good. Also, the jockey riding helps in making a decision. Daddy explained to me that you should never underestimate a "Longshot." They can be a threat to the main favorites. They have their purpose of being in this race. They are hungry, and they don't have anything to lose, so they are worth betting. They may bump coming out of the gate, but they keep running until they get to the finish line. If a Longshot is among the top 4 winners, that helps bring in the money. But, if he successfully comes in the first place, winning "The Run for the Roses," it will be an awesome payday! Hmm, what will I have when the transaction is over?

Don't be trapped by numbers. Especially if God is calling you, guiding you, and leading you to beat the odds. All you need is a little bit of faith when the odds are stacked up against you. Actually, with determination and God's help, you'll win. "What, then, shall we say in response to this? If God is for us, who can be against us?" (Rom 8:31 NIV). "I can do everything through him who gives me strength." (Phil 4:13 NIV).

Great, the bets placed, guests arrived, meat on the grill, smelling up the neighbor, sipping on Mint Juleps, everybody's partying and having a good time, waiting on that great Derby race to start. Now, let's jump to the race. The horses are in the starting gate, and they're off, going one and one-quarter miles around the track. Down the stretch on the inside rail, headed towards the finish line in 1st place at 50-1 odds, a Longshot, "Mine That Bird" with Calvin Borel. Wow, he was one of my Dad's favorite jockeys, that wins the Kentucky Derby on a muddy track, what a huge upset. A $2 bet paid out $103.20. In all his years of winning, this became the first year ever Daddy never cash a ticket, but I did. It was because of my Dad I decided to bet on that Longshot.

I didn't realize that 2009 would be my last year bonding with my Dad on a Kentucky Derby morning. Furthermore, later that year, my marriage falls apart. I would love my husband if he stayed, but I will survive him if he leaves. My journey enables me to walk alongside you, giving you that special touch of comfort, to ease the pain. I know you want the pain to go away, but the affliction serves a purpose. I know it's very hard to recognize purpose in your affliction. Nevertheless, my affliction leads me to my purpose, and my purpose is bigger than my pain.

I can identify the physical and emotional pain you are experiencing. And I can feel and understand your emotions, because of my afflictions and tear-stained path. I know firsthand the burdens you carry can be so hard to bear. Regardless, what you're going through, PUSH, do it no matter what. You can overcome adversity and recover from difficulties, challenges, and circumstances that have come against you. Bend through it. Rise above it. You got this, stop at nothing, hang in there until your change comes.

Don't give up. If you think you can. Then, what's stopping you? Faith works! Put it into action. If you think you can't, or you say "there's no way" come out your mouth, receive what you believe. Don't let what you feel affect what you say. Don't let what's temporary become a permanent fixture in your life. Again, what's stopping you?

Don't compare yourself to others. Be authentic! I will not be a poor copy of someone else, when I am "unique & wonderfully" made as to the original. Don't settle for a shadow, if you can be the light. Be secure in who God created you to be. Not everybody will celebrate your success, especially if your light shines brighter than theirs. So ask God for discernment. Remember, Judas was a close friend of Jesus, but he still betrayed him (Luke 22:4 NIV). Judas may seem like your friend right now, be all up in your face, but I'm certain, he will betray you, too.

As I rise through pain, my scars are the driving force to get me to the finish line.

"For the revelation awaits an appointed time; it speaks of the end and will not prove false. Though it lingers, wait for it; it will certainly come and will not delay." (Hab 2:3 NIV)

I'm a vessel of love God is using to reach out and touch His people. I began putting my pain on paper, which was therapeutic to me. I received healing through my writing. I will use my words as tools, to help lift people, instead of weapons, to bring people down. I want to be a blessing, and encourage someone who has lost his or her way, burden down with some much pain. Let these words enrich your life as you grow in Jesus.

Why not come and allow our heavenly Father, relieve you from carrying that heavy load? It's not His will for us to be burden down. God is there to support us, comfort us, strengthen us, love us, and use us, in unexpected ways. We must learn how to take our burden to the Lord and leave it there. He said to; "Cast your burdens to the Lord, and he will take care of you. He will not permit the godly to slip and fall." (Ps 55:22 NLT). "Come to me, all you who are weary and burdened, and I will give you rest. Take my yoke upon you and learn from me, for I am gentle and humble in heart, and you will find rest for your souls. For my yoke is easy, and my burden is light." (Matt 11:28-30 NIV).

As the journey continues for me, "Wheelchair Diva," I continue to push through some private pain that others have experienced. I attempt to address and find the root of problems that sometimes ignored. I realize how important prayer is and being in the Word of God daily will see you through, "Oh what a happy day it will be, to have no more pain.

If you do not give up, you will come up. So, never give up, never give in, and never lose hope. I had to let go of my load of fear getting up to walk. Also, denied by the insurance company, for a medication, that both of my doctors who specialize in Neurology, according to their expert opinion recommended. "Dr. Martin E. Brown" is an Assistant Professor, Department of Neurology / Co-Director, Division of Neuromuscular Medicine at the University of Louisville School of Medicine, here in Louisville, KY. & "Dr. Alan Pestronk" is a Professor, Departments of Neurology and Pathology & Immunology and the Director of the Neuromuscular Division / Neuromuscular Clinical Laboratory at Washington University School of Medicine in St. Louis, MO.

Administering "IVIG" & "Rituximab" was part of my medical plan, preparing me to be independent and walking in about 18 months. Certainly, they were very clear, and I understood that my walk would not be the same, but at least, I will be up walking. Immediately, I reminisce about becoming a "social butterfly" again.

Therefore, that was the missing piece of the puzzle, to stop this rare muscle disease, from attacking my muscles. Supposedly, would work well with other medications prescribed. More importantly, weaning me down to no longer take Steroids was part of the medical plan, as well. Steroids are a miracle drug, but they cause other problems, such as weight gain "OH MY GOODNESS." I don't understand it; approval received for "IVIG," but not "Rituximab." This medication was part of the medical plan designed for me. Rituximab would have a positive effect on my medical condition and functional ability. Why was it denied? As Tyson said, "Everyone has a plan until they get punched in the face.

"Many are the plans in a person's heart, but it is the Lord's purpose that prevails." (Prov 19:21 NIV).

The blow staggered us, but we're appealing the denial. Meanwhile, Medical necessity sent to support administering the drug "Rituximab." A Peer-to-Peer review is a next step when a preauthorization for services, been denied by the insurance company. In a peer review, professionals review each other's work to make sure it is accurate, relevant, and significant. The purpose of peer review is to improve the quality and safety of care.

However, the Appeal denied. How could this be? I felt punched in the gut, face, head, and my heart. I felt trapped in a dark valley. The enemy is trying to stop me, after denied several times, by my health insurance company. Peer review explained; "Rituximab" is a covered drug by the FDA for "Cancer," but not for "Myositis" (my diagnosis). It's considered experimental and experimental drugs not covered under my health insurance policy.

Anyways, I must step over my fears and grab it by faith. Despite your circumstances, do not fear. The Lord will be with us and guide us through troubled times. My specialists in their expert opinion would know how to treat me. You would think they have medical evidence that shows improvement in patients with the same diagnosis. God wouldn't bring me here if He didn't have a purpose for it. When all hell is breaking loose, keep calling on the Lord. Sometimes in the plan of God, things get worse before they get better. In spite of the adversities, hardships, circumstances we face, God is with us, even when there is no evidence He is. Put your trust in nobody, but Jesus. "Always pray and not give up" (Luke 18:1 NIV).

Suddenly, I felt the presence of God all over me. I didn't feel alone or afraid anymore. He promised in Psalms 23:4 (NIV) "Even though I walk through the darkest valleys, I will fear no evil, for you are with me; your rod and your staff, they comfort me." With that said, I decided not to worry, but trust. Not to be upset, but accept. I had confidence that I will see God's favor and His goodness in the land of the living.

Although my situation is tough, I refuse to let it steal my joy, my dreams, my hope, or my peace. No matter what the medical report says. I chose to focus on His promises operating in my life. God got me in the palm of His hands. I'm going to keep believing, keep trusting, keep hoping, always giving Him thanks, and praise His Holy Name. Because I'm "destined to win."

What's more, God can do the impossible. There is absolutely nothing too hard for Him. He can take nothing and turn it into something. When He speaks things change. He laid down His life, didn't anybody take it. He was crucified and resurrected. He can raise the dead. Heal the sick. Feed the hungry. Clothe the naked. Provide shelter during a storm. His angels will protect us. He'll give you double for your trouble. He loves us unconditionally. And He's always with us, never left us. Therefore, fear not, "Don't be afraid. Just stand still and watch the LORD rescue you today." (Exo 14:13 NLT). God is in control, and He's faithful. Therefore, no matter what comes your way, God is able, and He will see you through.

Let's go a step further. God is not limited to anything, but doubt. He made an iron ax-head float (2 Kings 6:6 NIV). A donkey talk (Num 22:28 NLT), and a corpse come back to life after four days (John 11 NIV). So rise and declare, "For nothing is impossible with God." (Luke 1:37 NLT)

Still, I was afraid of falling, but I kept getting up. Besides, it has been over three years since I walked on my own. My mind was moving faster than my body allowed. However, with assistance, I rise grabbing hold onto the walker and walked approximately 30 feet, but due to sideline cheers I got distracted and lost focus, then my left knee buckled, so I started stumbling, but I did not fall on the ground because I had protection all around me. At the same time, I wanted to give up and not try anymore.

Proverbs 4:25-27 (MSG) states, "Keep your eyes straight ahead; ignore all sideshow distractions. Watch your step, and the road will stretch out smooth before you. Look neither right nor left; leave evil in the dust." We must keep our eyes on the path in front of us, or we will stumble into sideline distractions that surround us. We do this by looking to Jesus.

God is anything and everything you need. At some point, you have to choose to release every adversity, care, concern, worry, doubt, fear, obstacles, circumstances, situations, issues, challenges, problems (whatever it may be), over to God into His loving hands. Like any damaged product, you must return to your manufacturer for repairs.

Just because you had a beat down, don't mean you won't have a great turnaround. There is a purpose for the pain. "Consider it pure joy, my brothers and sisters, whenever you face trials of many kinds because you know that the testing of your faith produces perseverance. Let perseverance finish its work so that you may be mature and complete, not lacking anything." (James 1:2-4 NIV)

How would you know God is a healer if you have never been sick? How would you know He's a provider, deliverer, a way maker, a protector, a heart fixer, a mind regulator if you never experience the need from Him to be any of these things? If we never go through anything, we would never know what God can do in, and through our lives.

I kept having faith and believing God didn't bring me this far to leave me. In fact, "He will restore my health." (Jer 30:17 NIV). I believe God would give me an "expected end" because He said He would. (Jer 29:11 KJV)). His promises taught me how to watch and pray to believe with faith, having thanksgiving in my heart that the Word of God will not fail" (Josh 21:45 NIV). Allow His peace to settle in your heart and mind, as you push through the pain; moving forward in your lane.

Everybody will go through something that will bring him or her down, on his or her knees. You need a friend who will stick with you through the bad times, someone who will support you, hang out with you, to encourage you when trouble comes, just to let you know, better days are coming.

What are you going to do when you face hurdles of adversity? Are you going to jump or stand there? The bible tells you that adversity will come, but God is the One who promises to lead us into victory. "A righteous man may have many troubles, but the Lord delivers him from them all." (Ps 34:19 NIV).

We can overcome every obstacle we face. "The Lord is my light and my salvation, so why should I be afraid? The Lord is my fortress, protecting me from danger, so why should I tremble? When evil people come to devour me, when my enemies and foes attack me, they will stumble and fall." (Ps 27:1-2 NLT)

Stay in faith. Put your hope and trust in God. He has promised that He is going to turn that difficulty around and use it for your advantage. Take joy in knowing that He created us with a purpose, for a purpose, on purpose, with a Divine plan that is good.

Satan, the enemy has been attacking all of us, and to tame that beast, is by the Word of God. The Word of God is our weapon. You can hit a bull's eye with it. Understand that God's Word is His will. When we pray according to God's will, we can have the confidence to receive what we have asked for, and live "Rejoicing always." (1Thess 5:16 NIV)

Taste and see that the Lord is good. Blessed is the one who takes refuge in Him! (Ps 34:8 NIV). When we get a taste of how God works in our lives, we are more prepared to wait with expectations for His plans for us to unfold. I trusted God when I didn't have results, and He turned it around and worked it out for me. In November 2018, "Polymyositis" went into remission, and weaned off steroids (Prednisone). Despite the fact, never being approved for, "Rituximab." God blessed me, regardless. I didn't need it, after all.

Also, since being in remission, I received inpatient aggressive therapy, at Frazier Rehab, to help wake my muscle so that I can walk. In fact, after 3 and ½ weeks of aggressive therapy, I got up with assistance and walked with a walker approximately 45 feet. I know you want to scream, "Won't He Do It" so go ahead, He's worthy of our praise! Now, praise him some more. Hallelujah! Give Glory to God!

I encourage you to pray, seek after Jesus to release that heavy load that's weighing you down. He wants you to cast those heavy burdens upon Him. "Pile your troubles on God's shoulders...he'll carry your load; he'll help you out. He'll never let good people topple into ruin." (Ps 55:22 MSG). Surely, God's highest wish is for us to be well.

3 John 1:2 (AMP) states, "Beloved, I pray that in every way you may succeed and prosper and be in good health [physically], just as [I know] your soul prospers [spiritually]." When it comes to the prayer, Jesus said, "Go into your room, close the door and pray to your Father, who is unseen. Then your Father, who sees what is done in secret, will reward you." (Matt 6:6 NIV).

You can pray anywhere, at any time: in your car, in the bathroom, lying in bed, while you're exercising, or at work. "Do not keep babbling like pagans, for they think they will be heard because of their many words. Do not be like them, for your Father knows what you need before you ask Him". (Matt 6:7-8 NIV). All God asks that we pray from our heart. Remember, this is our Father. Just keep it simple. Be spontaneous, personal, and honest. He knows better than us what we need.

Be committed to study & obey the Word of God. Let the Word renew your mind. Allow it to reshape your thoughts and your character.

Within these pages, you will discover the cause and effects of adversities and circumstances that cause all types of pain. However, don't lose heart. We can overcome anything with help from the Lord. Once more, I always pray and not give up.

The contents are to deliver a message of hope. Encourages you to hold steady. Empowers and enables you to let go of the pain held within. Motivates you to achieve peace. Hope restored. Influences to stay focused. Remain faithful. Keep believing, keep trusting, keep pushing, and keep moving forward until we see Jesus, "Oh, I must say, what a happy day it will be."

This book will inspire you and hopefully becomes a tool in leading you to the Word of God. There you will find joy. Are you discouraged today? Are you stressed out about something? Are you having health problems? Nevertheless, we can still have joy. We can have what Jesus called "my joy" if we ask Him. "For the joy of the Lord is our strength. (Neh 8:10 NIV). "I have told you this so that my joy may be in you and that your joy may be complete." (John 15:11 NIV) No Word. No joy.

Surely, have patience and faith in God. When you fully trust and believe in Him, you will enjoy "rest" He promised in Hebrews 4:3 (NLT) "For only we who believe can enter his rest." God can be trusted to keep His promises. He will never let us down.

This book is my gift to you "Let Go of the Load" Keep it close by my dear friend.

Poetry

Delivered & Set free through the Spoken Word

Being inspired by the "TIMES UP" movement;
our voices matter
Reminded me of my own story
Allow me to scale back and let the truth come
through
I'm giving it to you the way I see it, straight, no
chaser

<u>Times Up Rise Up</u>

Hey Sister
You Sister, You, You and You too
All my soul sisters
Do you have time for me?

Will you make time for me?
I need to talk to you my sister
If ya wondering what's up
Times up sister

To close those blinds my sister
The one you keep opening & closing
Aww yeah, see it, that one, right there

The one in the middle

With the monkey in the window
That gold mine you got
The one you keep opening and closing
That's what's up

You not alone my sister
Been there done that
Exposure brings closer
So, check this out

Being a naughty girl, up in a Penthouse Suite
Surrounded by seductions
Was encouraged to remove my shoes, after receiving Flowers, Chocolate Candy, Jewelry and a Beautiful Bottle of Perfume
Teased my mind, serving Mary Jane and the Finest Wine

Enticed with Designer Clothes, Red Bottom Shoes, Designer Purses had money in em too
Charmed with promises of good times and prosperity
Bribed with Wealth and Popularity
Inflamed my imagination to be exciting and calculating

Now, whatever I do, must be done exceptionally well
Be bold, not basic, and capable of being remembered
Confident, strong and unforgettable

So, I cast a spell with my performance
Had all his attention, and held on to it
Was so mesmerized made his nature rise
Very Irresistible

Enhanced my sexuality
He craved for my 'poo-nin-ney' but kept her out of reach
Making him want what I had to offer
Some of this Sweet & Tender Love

Began doing the splits and dropping it, because it's hot
Now give me what you got
Oh how sensational, so electrifying
He thought he had me, but no sister, had control, my sister

He shot off like a Roman candle
Shooting for the Stars
Strictly Business my sister

Focused and determined to get ahead
Successfully worked that Head
Earning my bread
To take care of the home, my sister

But enough is enough
Grasping for the material and the physical losing myself in the process
Being stuck, selling my soul, and not know what to do about it
Now I'm running to be away from it, and run right back into the very thing, I'm running from
You don't know how strong you are until you face something ugly
You must be willing to stand in your truth

Times Up, Rise Up

Sister, he thinks he has you, telling you, to use what you got, to get what you want
Oh really, then you made that booty clap
Very impressive, never seen it work like that before
He was captivated, stimulated and aroused

Been there, done that, but enough is enough, my sister
Times up, Rise up

Use your Creative Mind, and not that Energetic Behind

Sister, you are worth more than that
You are a treasure, something valuable, very special, classy beyond comparison, unique and you're precious
Sister come on, look at me, I'm reaching down to lift you up
We're better together than we are apart

Come on sister, reach out, take my hand, together we're stronger, we stand
Please, take my hand; you're not alone my sister

I know you think Dr. Feel-Good gives you all you need
But it ain't no way; you should continually be on your back or down on your knees to receive what you need
Is that how you lead your greatest asset, Mr. CEO?
By now, you should understand the seriousness of this situation
You're an animal. Very wicked, sneaky and cunning to get what he wants.

Times up, rise up; sister don't you know you are a primary Stakeholder
Your actions can affect the outcome of this company
You've started from the bottom now you here
Prepared, Equipped, and Qualified
Come on my sister; enough is enough

Don't tolerate things that come from the devil. Let go of guilt, the shame, the fear, manipulation, and intimidation. Don't let it paralyze you. Go to God. He will forgive you and restore you everything the devil tries to take away from you.

Sister, come out, come out, wherever you are
Sister, I see you, look up, come on, get up, come on
Times Up, Rise Up

Take my hand together we stand
You're not alone my sister
Been there, done that
Now I'm Free

You see, there was a time in my life I had a side hustle. I had bills and two kids to care for. I wanted to live lavish and look extravagant. So, I went into survivor mode and did what I had to do to make ends meet. Finally, in between hustles, it was as if a light bulb went off. I woke up after hearing and receiving the Word of God. "And my God shall supply all your need according to His riches in glory by Christ Jesus." (Phil 4:19NKJV)). I've learned to be content, satisfied, and happy because I have Jesus. He is with me. I wanted to see the kind of woman I knew I was.

Furthermore, in Matthew 6:33 (NIV). "But seek first his kingdom and his righteousness, and all these things will be given to you as well." Then, I began to Tithe. I experienced an increase. Therefore, motivation and determination kicked in. Surely, there's no doubt the Word of God is true. Trust in His promises. I'm demonstrating to you what I come to believe & know to be true. As a child of God, I know with Him, I got the victory. I had to face reality. More to the point, I love me better than that.

"If you want to be a woman in power, then empower other women." (Nina Shaw).

My Voice for a friend through Spoken Word

Inspired by "Me Too" a movement against sexual harassment and sexual assault Highlights Top Dogs only if the shoe fits. How you treat others, especially when you are in a position of power, determines how God will treat you.

The way I see it:

<u>CEO #CE Hoe</u>

This how you do business
You call and say come to my office
Shut and lock the door
Time for my lap dance

How professional is that
You a hoe don't you know
Then you want to be, pleased
Push her down on her knees

Achieve what you need

How professional is that
You a hoe don't you know
You have lust in your heart
Right from the start
Next, you want her best part
You pull up her dress

Pinned the panties to your chest
Bend her across your desk
How professional is that
You a hoe don't you know

Listen I say, Mr. CEO
You a hoe don't you know
Your day has come for you to
Hit the door and go, you hoe

I bet you won't be back
No more, No more
There's a place for a hoe
Don't you know?

Now you bend over
Behind the door or be on the floor
Rather achieve on your knees
Aren't you willing to please?

Now you see you rather be free
You like being a hoe
Don't you know Mr. CEO?

Ladies, I stand in the gap praying for you, thanking the Lord, for rescuing you and restore you. When God restores, He puts things together in the right way. Don't be intimidated by your enemies. Remember this, More Than Conquerors. "What, then, shall we say in response to these things? If God is for us, who can be against us? (Rom 8:31 NIV) Nothing can stand against God. Get to a place where you are fully persuaded to trust God. He's the reason to be down on your knees so that you can remain on your feet. "Everything I am; I owe to God. Everything I have comes from God. And all belong to Him. To God, be all the glory."

Abuse of any kind is wrong. Come out of the shadows and tell your story. Help the voiceless. Shed off the bondage and come to have the peace, only God can bring. Let me leave you with this; it cost something to be a survivor. Be strong and courageous. We are to persistently, bring our prayers before God. Pray for justice. "And will not God bring out justice for His chosen ones, who cry out to Him day and night? Will He keep putting them off?" Justice is coming.

"One thing stays constant…Telling the truth. You must be present at the table, giving your perspective." (Gayle King)

Understanding Life's Trials

"Take delight in the Lord, and he will give you your heart's desires." (Ps 37:4 NLT)

To anyone who has lost hope in whatever you believe God for, I encourage you to keep on believing because God can do the impossible — diagnosed with a rare muscle disease called Polymyositis. Its name means inflammation of many muscles, causing muscle weakness affecting both sides of your body. It's an Autoimmune disease. Having this condition have made it difficult to walk, climb stairs, rise from a seated position, lift objects, or reach overhead.

Research shows Polymyositis is more common in blacks than in whites, and women are affected more than men are. It goes on to say adults in their 30s, 40s or 50s most commonly affected. Signs and symptoms usually develop gradually, over weeks or months, because it is constantly being undiagnosed and overlooked.

Furthermore, it is not known for sure how many have myositis. According to the most recent analysis from the Myositis Association patients report, it takes 3 ½ years and nearly five doctors to receive a correct autoimmune disease diagnosis. There is a great deal of damage done to the muscles during this wait time. I had symptoms for three years before a doctor said Myositis. Bringing public awareness of the disease increases the chances of positive patient outcomes. They say there is no cure for myositis, but I will remain hopeful that a cure and the cause gets discovered.

However, there's a treatment that can improve muscle strength and function. The earlier treatment started, the more effective it is. The hardest lesson for me is to accept the things I cannot change. My biggest discovery since being disabled and limited to a wheelchair, God is who He says He is. Although having this condition for almost three and 1/2 years, my husband still takes care of me.

However, I found myself having to remind him of our wedding vows. He said, "We are better together than we are apart. Once again, "I'm to love you if you stay with me, and I'm strong enough to survive you if you leave me." Still, he insisted that he wasn't going anywhere and he's going to take care of me because he loves me. He misses me, and he wants us back, the way we use to be. And I do too.

In the meantime, I discovered that I'm able to deal with things; I never thought I would be able to do. When you do all you can, you stand. Besides, with strength; I'm armed for this battle. This social butterfly has slowed down and has given all my attention in seeking God and fulfilling the plans he has for me. God will take care of my husband. I will stay in peace, which is a position of power, and see the deliverance of the Lord. God operates, secretly, quietly, but surely.

What do you do when you don't know what to do? Do you need a miracle? Do you need something that seems so impossible that only God can handle? Just pray. God is powerful. He can take nothing and turn it into something. He can make a way when there seems to be no other way. He can speak light in your darkest hour; speak hope into hopeless situations and broken dreams.

More importantly, give Him your praise. When you praise God in your darkest hour, when you praise Him when things seem to be too much to handle, and you still praising Him when you feel completely trapped by circumstances, and all your hope is gone, that's when God enters in your situation. Praise moves God to intervene. Decide to praise God when facing adversity; you can't handle. Embrace it. Within adversity, lies opportunity. When things look hopeless, remember, Jesus looked at them and said, "With man, this is impossible, but not with God; all things are possible with God." (Mark 10:27 NIV). When you think you can't, remember to say, "I can do everything through Christ, who gives me strength." (Phil 4:13 NLT).

You may not feel able, but He is. Remind yourself and say, "My God is able." There's nothing too hard for Him. Remind God of His promises. And watch Him work. Stay focus on Him instead of the problem. Do what the Lord wants. He got you. "Though he may stumble, he will not fall, for the Lord upholds him with his hand." (Ps 37:24 NIV). He will intentionally become involved in your situation, to make it work out for your good.

It was November 2018, when this rare muscle disease (Polymyositis) went into remission. Later, admitted into Frazier Rehab (January 2019) to receive aggressive physical therapy, to wake my muscles up. Then in February, after 3 ½ weeks of therapy, I walked 45 feet with a Walker; let me remind you, I have not walked since 2015. All around me, with my wheelchair close by for safety purposes, three therapists.

Presently, I'm attending outpatient therapy at Frazier Rehab twice a week to improve weakness in my proximal muscles (hips, thighs, shoulders, and arms). I still have ways to go, but I'm hopeful better days are coming. Aneta, you stepped in when Christie's off. Thank you for listening when my heart was heavy. Your encouragement gave me the strength to keep fighting and keep believing in myself. Christie and Livy, you both are a great therapist. You have the skills and equipment to treat my condition and get me back on my feet again. I'm so grateful.

Words cannot articulate how much I appreciated the love I received from Kristen, Frannie, and Tamikko. Also, to all my CNA's, my nurses, and my wonderful doctors; Dr. Sarah Wagers (doctor of physical therapy) and Dr. Martin Brown (specialist in myositis). There are not enough words to express gratitude; I have within me. Inpatient at Frazier Rehab, I witnessed the hand of God working through every Therapist, Doctor, and Patient. God is a healer.

For every setback, God already has a comeback. For every disappointment, He has restoration. For every injustice, He has vindication. For that betrayal that seems to be working against you, God knows how to turn it around and cause it to work for you.

I encourage you to praise God no matter what because He is praiseworthy and credible. Praise Him for what is due to Him, to get what you want Him to do for you, and if nobody else praises God, you praise Him all by yourself.

"Father God, I stand in awe as I praise you. Thank you for just being you. Thank you for your faithfulness. You are so good to us. You are great and magnificent. Lord, we praise you and thank you for your grace and your mercy, in Jesus name." Amen.

I will not let my pride or my arrogance stop me from worshipping and praising God. I chose to trust even though I do not understand the adversity that has come upon me.

Wheelchair Diva continues to stay focused, as she pushes through the pain of becoming independent, and the ability to walk on her own. She continues to hold on to her faith, as she keeps moving forward in her lane.

There are times when stress and frustration come having to depend on others, especially family members. Because family members who are caregivers get fatigued and burnout, this wears down their capacity for compassion. And, when you add clashing personalities to the mix, conflicts are almost bound to happen.

How you respond depends on the situation. At that moment, you end up frustrated, angry, and sad. Then you and your loved ones suffer. Therefore, my role as the person receiving the care chooses to offer genuine praise. I make it clear how much I appreciate the care given to me. I recognize that their bucket may feel empty at times, and it needs replenishing. I make it my business to practice compassion, allowing them to vent when they feel overwhelmed because holding in feelings can result in growing frustration.

Furthermore, I often notice people put caregivers on a pedestal, but they can be nasty and grouchy, too, being tired of caring for you. With that said, the person who is disabled would love for you to trade places with them, then maybe the caregiver would be more empathetic, kind-hearted and compassionate.

However, they need more love and encouragement too, because they are required to give more love away. For this, I am extremely grateful. All is well, and all will be well. God is so much bigger than anything you will face. Leave everything in the palm of His hands with assurance that He will take care of you. So, smile even though you have been going through it for a while. Still, keep on smiling, knowing God is behind the scenes working things out for you. Surely, this too shall pass, but it would be good if it happens now, let us pray.

Father, you are aware of everything, and I know you see the struggles in my heart. Problems you already know that I still need to share with you. They are painful, and I do not want to make a mistake feeding into it. Therefore, I choose to unfasten, release, and let go of the struggles in my heart that I do not understand. And Father, I praise you and thank you for peace I found in Psalms 31:7 (NIV) that says, "I will be glad and rejoice in your unfailing love, for you have seen my troubles, and you care about the anguish of my soul."

More to the point, Psalms 46:1 (NLT) states, "God is our refuge and strength, always ready to help in times of trouble." Oh how comforting to know that when trouble comes, I can seek shelter in You and you will protect me. In Jesus name, Amen.

Life is going to throw you curveballs. You can't always avoid them. Face it head-on. Embrace it to see how it can make your life better. You may not understand everything that is going on in your life, but God has a plan to take every problem you face and turn it around and use it to bring you good because He loves you. Just know "that in all things God works for the good of those who love him, who have been called according to his purpose." (Rom 8:28 NIV)

Remember, those things you are facing are only temporary. Besides, you have seen God's goodness in the past, and He has something big in store for you in your future. Wait patiently for Him. Waiting is not one of my strongest suits, but the outcome is well worth the wait. The appointed time is the best. So, be patient and wait on God's timing. It is always right and always perfect. Likewise, at that set time, everything God promised will happen. So you might as well get ready to receive his goodness because He is faithful. Stay in faith; keep doing the right thing and put your trust in Him.

Hidden Figures

If you sense something is off, don't ignore the warning signs. I had a feeling my girlfriend had something going on, but I just cannot put my finger on it.

On this particular day, I wore Fire Engine Red fingernail polish, a wide Fedora Black Brim, Calf high boots, and Fishnet pantyhose. Above the knee, form-fitting black/white Tadashi suit, with beautiful Diamond and Pearls jewelry on, looking fly and feeling glamorous, just for me. Oh, and by the way, I smelled amazing with a little EAU DE PARFUM by "Alien."

I enjoy dressing up and looking like I am blessed. Feeling amazing and looking sexy for my man. You have to be bold and not basic, to get noticed. Be playful; having a sense of humor makes you more desirable. You must grab attention and hold on to it. You must be memorable, captivating, and unforgettable. Be unique. Brand-new. Be different. Sweep them off their feet. Be so irresistible that they crave your smell. Be capable of being remembered. Always behave like a woman and not act needy. Respect yourself, and you will get respect.

These words of wisdom I will always remember that came from my aunties and my girlfriends who are older than me. It is always fun exploring ways to keep it hot for your significant other. The thought came to mind to come up with a marketing strategy to sell vaginal cream and adult toys. Both will enhance your sexual appetite. So, I planned a fantasy party. I knew it would sell well because I tried the toys and the cream myself and loved it! I wanted to be bold, think outside the box, ensuring enjoyment, having an unforgettable party, while selling products I wanted my friends to enjoy.

Since, I know how women shop, we buy with our eyes and we are the world's most powerful consumers, an idea came to mind. I decided to call a good friend who had a side hustle, as a stripper, (Sexy Chocolate) to join me in planning, an unforgettable fantasy party at his house. He is simply amazing. He had a gorgeous smile, beautiful teeth, handsome and built. Muscular with a six-pack and Bowlegged. You cannot help but touch him. We thought about rubbing him down in baby oil, dressed only in a G-string. And barefooted.

So, the party started at 7 pm, and at midnight, the party was still going strong. We sold out of the vaginal cream with sales pending. Even my "holy roller" friends had it raining dollar bills all over.

Oh, what an enjoyable, unforgettable party. In between performances, I noticed one of my girlfriends sneaking Sexy Chocolate into the bathroom. Then, they went into the master bedroom. I knew she had the hots for him. My gut told me so, but that is none of my business. Come to find out, that's her secret lover, what a small world. However, we sold out of the entire product displayed on silver meat platters. They had a great appetite. "Laugh out loud." I must plan another real soon after asked on numerous occasions. Just keeping it real.

It's Just Like That

Having a baby to hold onto a man, but he still doesn't want you. Oh, what about, you love a man that has a love for another woman. Has this ever happen to you? Would you settle for this? The devil is a liar!

In Genesis 29:1-35 (NIV) is a complicated story about an older sister (Leah) who marries a man (Jacob), but loved her younger sister (Rachel) a shepherd, instead. In Genesis 27:41-46 (NIV) Jacob arrived in Harran, after he fled from home, fearing his twin brother, Esau, was going to kill him. Meanwhile, he happens to run into Rachel as she is about to water Laban's flocks, who's her father and Jacob mother's brother. She was beautiful, and he fell in love with Rachel, Laban's younger daughter. Jacob wanted to marry Rachel, but it would come with a price.

Jacob had to work as a shepherd for seven years, tending to Laban's flocks. Laban deceived Jacob and gave Rachel's older sister, Leah, to him as his wife. Jacob didn't want to go for that. But Laban argued that it wasn't custom to give the younger daughter in marriage first. So Jacob and Leah had to stay married for seven years and still tend to Laban's flocks before he could marry Rachel.

So, after fourteen years of labor, Jacob had two wives. Leah and Rachel. Leah longed for the love from her husband, but he loved Rachel and showed her favoritism. Leah craved for this man and even conceived six sons and a daughter by him, but it didn't matter, because he would rather be with Rachel whom he truly loved. Rachel had two sons by Jacob. However, tragedy struck, and she died giving birth to her second son. So sad, Leah trying to gain approval or acceptance from her husband, that had a love for somebody else.

You try to pursue a man by having babies. What good did it do for you? You still alone all by yourself with a bunch of kids. How many women do you know who fits this same scenario? Trying to trap a man, so you get pregnant, thinking he's going to stay with you. He still leaves you, and there he goes to be with somebody else, having kids by them. Don't even take care of the kids he has by you, and "It's just like that." Still, it doesn't matter who left you. It matters who's with you. That's the Lord.

But through the birth of her children, Leah realized that it was the Lord, she should be pursuing. So, after giving birth to her last child, she even said, "This time I will praise the Lord." She stopped having children by a man that loved another woman. We must take control and be responsible for our happiness. Let go of the load. Humble yourself and climb into God's Word. Regain strength. Receive His goodness and faithfulness. Keep trusting Him. Surrender to His unconditional love. Expect good things to happen for you. One touch of God's favor can accelerate you higher than you can ever imagine. Have a made up mind to enjoy your life. See the brighter side of your circumstances. Permit yourself to be happy. Jesus will take care of you. God is still on the throne. He is behind the scenes working things out for you.

Judging and Repentance

Are there any sins you committed you have not been honest with God about? Have you ever cheated on your tax returns? Have you ever called in sick when you weren't? Have you ever cheated on your spouse or a significant other? Did you tear down someone else's character to make yourself look better? Don't lie. Be honest. Tell the truth it will set you free. Pursue truth. Walk in it.

In Isaiah 1, God confronts His people about wrongs they'd committed. Even then God responded mercifully, asking the people of Judah to confess what they'd done and turn from it. God is sovereign. He longs for us to be open and honest with Him. "If we confess our sins, he is faithful and just and will forgive us our sins and purify us from all unrighteousness." (1 John 1:9)

Have you ever done something that seems to be right at the time, not intending to do any harm, but later came back to bite you? I don't have the right to be judgmental if I consider myself, because I'm not perfect, either! I have done some things myself, so who am I to judge. I had to ask Jesus to forgive me and to help me to do better. So allow me to take this time to ask for forgiveness for any pain I caused to any of my relatives and friends. I'm so sorry for my actions; please forgive me.

"Do not judge, or you too will be judged. For in the same way you judge others, you will be judged, and with the measure you use, it will be measured to you." (Matt 7:1-2 NIV).

But, everyone judges others unfairly and harshly. We complain and say unkind words to others. The Word says, "He who conceals hatred has lying lips, and he who spreads slander is a fool" (Prov 10:18 NIV). "For all have sinned, and fall short of the glory of God." (Rom 3:23 NIV). "We all, like sheep, have gone astray, each of us has turned to his own way, and the LORD has laid on him the iniquity of us all." (Isa 53:6 NIV).

We all have said unkind things and done unkind things that seem right at the time. So when you think back, you will be amazed to see how much God has forgiven you for sins known & unknown. In turn, you need to show forgiveness, as well. Be wise and give God glory.

Bitterness

Are you bitter about something? Release it. Bitterness will follow you everywhere you go. Bitter people are hard to deal with, and they are very unpleasant. They destroy relationships. They are very negative. They walk around with a chip on their shoulder. They have inner hurt and anger. They carry their emotions on their sleeves. They want you to read their mind. They are ruthless. Have a sharp tongue and say things to hurt people's feelings. It's all about them. They are selfish, uncaring, insensitive, and vengeful.

We must guard our hearts against bitterness. Your words show where your heart is. The bible says, "For the mouth speaks what the heart is full of." (Matt 12:34 NIV).

Do not hold on to grudges. Ask God to help you to get over the anger you have in your heart. Surrender, forgive, and let go of what is in your heart that has been eating away at you. Pray for the person who has hurt you to overcome bitterness. "Get rid of all bitterness, rage and anger, brawling, and slander, along with every form of malice. Be kind and compassionate to one another, forgiving each other, just as Christ Jesus forgave you." (Eph 4:31-32 NIV). The Word of God goes on to say, "Make every effort to live in peace with everyone and to be holy; without holiness, no one will see the Lord. See to it that no one falls short of the grace of God and that no bitter root grows up to cause trouble and defile many." (Heb 12:14-15 NIV)

Domestic Abuse

Can you believe that someone you love, that claims to love you, verbally, mentally and physically abused you? Have you ever been out in public, being yelled at, trying to control you, humiliating and embarrassing you, in front of people? Did he ever try to manipulate your emotions and made you feel guilty? Have you ever left him and find yourself back with him, because the sex was so good?

This pain started slowly. We shacked up for about five years. My partner began to blame me for things I didn't have control of; he would pick at my faults. He started being jealous. I was feeling trapped and miserable, and I couldn't see any way out. I felt unsafe, so I moved a lot, but my family & friends did not understand why I moved so much. They talked about me saying things like, "Every time I turn around, she's always moving, living like a gypsy." I couldn't tell them the man I was living with was stalking me. We would break up, then here he comes back crying, begging and apologizing, I forgive him, and let him back in. He used money and sex to control me, to keep me from leaving him.

For that reason, he gets back in and treats me very well for a quite a while, then starts acting like a fool again. He became extremely jealous, questioning me where I've been. Accuse me of flirting with other men, jealous of the time I spend with my girlfriends, even with my family. Constantly, calling me at work, and dropping by my job, unexpectedly. He blamed me for everything. He never took responsibility for his problems. He would blow things out of proportion, took everything personally. He became very angry and explosive. He started bullying me and mentally and physically abusing me. He told me, "If I tried to leave him, he was going to kill me."

I had enough. I wanted this relationship to be over; I wasn't going to take it anymore; done hit me one time too many and said, "If I can't have you won't nobody have you. I'm going to kill you, bitch."

Therefore, on this particular day, we were arguing and fighting. I was tearing his ass up. He had been drinking and was drunk and high, after sniffing lines of cocaine. I hit him with an iron skillet and a straightening comb. He was able to grab me, knocked me down, and then he pulled out his gun, put it up to my head, pull the trigger, but the gun jammed. "Hallelujah" that was nobody but the Lord on my side. Somehow, I was able to get away. I was so afraid for my life, and my children were there too.

Meanwhile, I grabbed up my kids and ran to my neighbor's house who called the police, when the police arrived, they saw all the bruises and scars, a black eye and a busted lip. They suggested that I go to the hospital, but I declined. They followed me home, but he had long gone. They advised me to take out an Emergency Protection Order (EPO) out on him, so when they catch him, they'll lock him up, but it didn't do any good. He would call me, come to my house beat on the door. I would call the police, but when they got there, he had gone.

So, this went on for a couple of years. I moved from pillar to post, no matter where I moved to, that man would find me. He would be outside my home, my job, my kid's school, the babysitter's house, and the grocery store. I would see him going through the alley when visiting my parents. It just didn't matter.

One Sunday, when leaving the church, I noticed my car windows were busted out. I was so embarrassed. The police came and took a report. It was obvious that my car was the only one targeted. So, they ask, if I was having problems with anybody and I told them, YES, I had an EPO out on him and gave his name. I told them about him stalking me and torturing me. And how it's become a complete nightmare. No one could ever understand the inner torture he caused me. It agonized me for days wondering when it was going to be the next time he does something else. I knew he done it because he called me the night before, and I ignored all his calls.

His actions have gotten extreme. At that time, I attended Calvary East United Methodist Church, where Rev. Leonard Johnson was the Pastor. He was concerned for my safety. He prayed for me and said, "Daughter you got those kids, and you need to tell somebody what you are going through. This matter has gotten out of control. Anytime, a person comes on your church's parking lot to vandalize your car; he needed to be stopped, by any means necessary."

I was so afraid I didn't want my father, or my brothers involved. I was embarrassed to tell anybody what I was going through. I ended all communications after he attempted to contact me on numerous occasions.

My job knew something was going on with me because he kept calling me at work. When my productivity started going down, they started questioning me about things going on at home. They knew something wasn't right after he kept making emergency calls all the time. I just told them, "I'm stressed out." I was afraid to tell anyone what I was going through. I began losing weight, my hair started shedding and falling out, got behind in my bills, couldn't sleep, kept a stomachache, then started having pains in my chest, neck, and back. My kids didn't understand what was going on with me.

I would call the police, but it didn't matter, so I took matters in my own hands. Therefore, I told my dad's friend, Osborne a police officer at that time, what I was going through, and I told my uncle, "Radio" about it and he said, "You ain't running no more, that "MF" is going to make me kill 'em. I got something for that ass". So, he gave me a gun for my protection. That was the day all my fear was gone. I started thinking about every time he hit me, cursed me out, bullied me, stalked me, intimidated me, embarrassed me, ignited fire I had inside me. I wasn't taking it anymore. I cried out, "Lord, I can't defeat this devil on my own, but I know you can, so I'm trusting you to take care of me."

Then it happens, he had the nerve to block me in my driveway, as I was leaving for work one morning with my kids in the car. I was on my way to drop them off at the babysitter's house. I decided I was going to gain control of my life. He knew I'd taken an EPO out on him because they went on his job and locked him up. We went to court, and they told him to stay so many feet away from me. Do not have any contact with me, if so, he was going to jail. It didn't matter; he's been there before. He gotten out of his car began verbally abusing me. I told my kids to lay down in the back seat and do not move. I reached in my purse, got out of the car with my 38 aimed at him, cocked and ready to fire. I went gangster on him. I told him to get the "F..." away from here, I'm not scared of you, I don't want you, I got me somebody else in my life, and ya not going to run him off, on this day you are going to respect me. Come on; I dare you, say something else smart, now take another step and make my day, your family will be burying you. He said, "Awe, it's like that now, you don't want me no more; you are going to shoot me." I said, try me. "He said, "I hear ya, I'm gone, I'll leave you alone."

Then he left, and he never bothers me again. When I showed that devil that I was not taking it anymore, that enough is enough, I'm not running anymore; there's no more fear here. He left me alone. I praise God for his hand of protection over my life.

However, a few months later, he sends a letter in the mail apologizing, using the lyrics to Maze featuring Frankie Beverly, "Can't Get Over You." I know I brought it on myself. I owe no blame to no one else. And I realize I can't get over you. And though I do my very best, I just can't find happiness, and it's all because I can't get over you. Hey baby, why oh why, thinking of you makes me cry, no matter how I try, I'm gonna love you, bye and bye, I don't know what to do, I can't get over you. I guess you'll always have a part somewhere deep in my heart; it's just hard to hide I can't get over you. I tried to lose myself in song, but the ties are much too strong, what I'm going to do I can't get over you. It makes me feel so bad, messing up the love we had, there's one thing I know, I will always love you so.

Boy Bye! There was a time when I truly can say, I had this song in my heart for him, a song by my girl, Aretha Franklin, "I ain't never loved a man the way that I loved you." However, I often thought while I was in this abusive state, it's been a long time coming, but I know, "A change is gonna come" (Sam Cooke).

Once more, abuse of any kind is wrong. Don't be a doormat, accepting abuse, as it is normal even if you're getting your basic needs met. Still, don't accept being abused. Make a decision that you want better for yourself. I pray whoever is presently going through any Domestic Violence this prayer from Devon Franklin will encourage you to do something.

"Dear Lord, I accept that there are things I have had to endure that I may never understand. I ask you for healing emotionally, mentally, physically, and spiritually. Please give me comfort in the times when discomfort is the only feeling available to me. I accept that you have created me for greatness, and I commit myself to pursue it every day. I accept that there are some men who cannot handle all you have created me to be. But I will not make myself smaller to fit into their limited view of who I am! I no longer accept any man who can't respect me! I no longer accept anyone who tries to make me feel inferior! I no longer accept feelings of insecurity or lack of self-worth! I accept the fullness of my calling and destiny! I accept the power of the woman you have created me to be! I will not live quietly; I roar with the excellence and authority you have given me from this day forward!"

"In the mighty name of Jesus, Amen!"

Depression

Depression is a result of something external. It is external pressures on the outside getting on the inside, weighing you down. It is stress and pressure internalized, gets into your heart, and weighing you down. It is the feelings that come from thinking thoughts that's been weighing you down.

What are you exposing yourself to, that's causing you to have this negative thinking? And what are you thinking? If you change your thinking, you can change how you feel. The devil is after your destiny. Depression is a tool Satan uses to keep the will of God from your life. The Word of God is the tool God uses to change the way of thinking to bring success in your life. But we constantly go elsewhere looking for substitutes trying to replace God. We go to someone else, drink alcohol, smoke weed, want money, go shopping, to name a few. God is the best choice to be free from depression. (Creflo Dollar)

Have you replaced God? Are you depressed because somebody walked away? Quit being sour because somebody walked out and left you. Let them go. You don't want anybody who doesn't want you. If they were supposed to be for you, they never would have left you. There is somebody perfectly design just for you. Depression in some form will touch each of us at some point in life. Whether your depression is caused by losing things you love, or being overwhelmed by the pressures of responsibility, or feeling drained after having great success. You must turn to God our Great Physician and let Him make you whole again.

When you put your trust in God and begin to praise Him, depressions lift, and hope returns. The bible says in 1 Peter 5:7 (AMP), "Casting all your cares...all your anxieties, all your worries, and all your concerns, once and for all…on Him, for He cares about you with the deepest affection, and watches over you very carefully."

Addiction

Be selective about the company you keep. "Do not be misled: Bad company corrupts good character." (1 Cor 15:33 NIV). They can drag you down.

I realized my son needed help. I had no idea where to begin. It is a process to get clean and stay clean. He would get off the drugs and alcohol then get back on. It seems I wanted him to be clean more than he wanted for himself. I would tell him that he needed to change the people in his circle. The company that you keep influences your conduct. They have to want it more than you want it for them.

Unbelievably, his Dad and I had gotten to the point that we wanted him to be locked up, so he would get off these streets, at least we would know where he's at and be able to sleep at night. Every time we hear the news that another black man found dead, we often wonder if it was he. We felt overwhelmed.

I had permitted him to drive my car, to get back and forth to work so that he can take care of his son. Later, the car gets vandalized. In other words, shot up, deemed a totaled loss. At the time, I was in the hospital, not knowing if he was in the car or not. I pray for my son both day and night. Lord, save my son, reveal yourself to him in a personal and intimate way. I know you can save him in a crack house. Have him to understand he is not in this world alone. Thank you for commanding Your angels to be around him, protecting him in all his ways.

I must have patience. Sometimes the best thing to do is nothing. God can make things happen when it seems impossible. Only God raises the dead. Believe what the Word of God says, "Be still and know that I am God." (Ps 46:10 NIV).

Finally, I heard from him. But the drama continued he has to admit to himself that his life is unmanageable, and he has to turn it over to a power higher than himself. What I understood that would be his first step. So, the only thing I could do was pray with boldness asking God to deliver him, help him, and restore him, one more time. He needs to learn how to receive God's mercy and let go of guilt and shame. I believe God is answering my prayers, and it's finished. I know he has had several setbacks, but God's mercy is bigger than any mistakes we have made. Later, I received a letter from my son releasing pain held within.

Ronnie writes, "Dear Mama, this story isn't like most story's you hear. My name is Ronnie

McWhorter. I'm from Louisville, Kentucky. State of the "Bluegrass." Home of the Hustlers, Pimps, and Kingpins. All those names sound good, being where I've been. Now I'm older. I think those names have changed quite a bit. Through all my ups and downs, my friends and loved ones, anyone who has come in contact with this soul of a man has been disappointed and let down. Nothing good has happened for me, except, having my son, JaCarie.

Above all, he's the one that I let down the most. Lost was with no means of finding my way to dry land. I was drowning in my pool of pain and self-pity and having self-imposed crisis from the action I put forth.

On this day, 12-11-18, something happens, and everything in my life changed. Not only was it my Mama's birthday, but I found the power to go on. Here's my story in finding the power.

As far as I can remember, I never thought I was good enough. It wasn't because I wasn't getting love from my family. I always felt like something was missing. So, I lived through other people's accomplishments. Daydreaming, wishing they were mine, hoping that one day, my luck would change. Hopefully, it happens soon. But that thought soon sailed away and wouldn't return for many years.

As a young man, I went through many depressing days. I wasn't even a teenager yet when I had my first drink. Safe to say, I didn't like it, but everyone in my school was doing it. I just wanted to fit in, so I did it, too. But, that didn't last too long because I was introduced to weed. That day my whole life changed.

Everything that made me sad, angry, depressed, or afraid went away. I felt like that was the missing piece I was looking for been found. This feeling only lasted for 30 minutes to an hour. Then I went back to that lonely, afraid, little boy that I hated. I had to find me again. Then, I vowed that I wouldn't go another day without it. My mother and father had no idea what I was going through. They only saw what I allowed them to see. I lied, cheated, and even stole to stay high because I never wanted to feel that pain I felt before to enter my body again. I could hide it pretty well. Back then, weed was so cheap, never in a million years did I think I had a problem.

However, this went on for several years until that day; I had my first encounter with Louisville Police. I was 17 years old. I figured they would slap me on my wrist and put me in rehab. My first encounter with AA (alcohol anonymous) was in 1999 at a place called Ten Brook. The kids there were well off and ungrateful. Their parents were Doctors and

Lawyers. These kids were doing drugs I never heard before, like, Heroin and Meth. I was like, "What the hell is that?" I only do weed, saying that to myself. If my parents where Lawyers and Doctors, I wouldn't even smoke cigarettes. I was so much in denial that; I couldn't even stop smoking weed to pass the urine test we had every Wednesday. I found a way to cheat the test and done it very well. Even graduated from the program faster than everyone else by lying and cheating and not knowing that what I was doing would bite me in the ass later on.

It wasn't long after leaving the program that I found Cocaine. From then on, me and her (cocaine) were together, but the things I have done to keep her around was so bad that my whole personality changed to the point I went from being happy what weed did for me, to hating everyone and everything. I didn't know why at the time, but I never thought it was cocaine. I only wanted to be noticed when I started getting high.

Then I only wanted peace. Something cocaine wouldn't allow me to have. She (cocaine), took all the ambitions that I obtain through other people's accomplishments to only wanting her and nothing else. So, for the next 20 years, I would be going in and out of rehab. And in and out of prison. Losing friends and loved ones and several material things didn't matter to me, anyway. My whole life was in shambles. I was so far down there was nowhere else to go, but up.

I met so many people on this journey. But there's one who stands out more than anyone else that said something to me that made a whole lot of sense. "How powerless my life is, is how unmanageable my living was? To me, he looked like a man with all the answers. So, I had a question for him. "How do I find that power?"

All my life I've done nothing but things that would take me further from the Man I know that can fix all problems. That man is God. I've been searching for Him all my life.

When I think back, it was at the beginning I said there was always something missing. I never would believe something that I couldn't see would be able to fix me. It was hard for me to get over that hurdle. The pain had gotten so great that I was willing to believe in anything. This man God sent in my life, showed me how to pray, and he showed me what willingness was.   I'm truly grateful that God didn't give up on me with all I've done. He's given me another chance, a new start. Another beginning. And I can't wait to see what else God has in store for me. This power is accessible to you, only if you believe in a power greater than you do. God Bless you, Ronnie.

The bible states to "Be alert and of sober mind. Be self-controlled and watchful." Your adversary, the devil, prowls around like a roaring lion looking for someone to devour".

(1 Peter 5:8 NIV).

We're called to be attentive and alert because we have a very real enemy lurking around. If your life is ineffective and depressed or unproductive and stagnant, look at the people you've surrounded. Misery loves company, so steer clear of negative thinking people. They will drag you down with them.

"We all face disappointments and setbacks, but if we're going to see God's best, we have to have a bounce-back mentality. That means when you get knocked down, you don't stay down. You get back up again. You have to know that every time adversity comes against you, it's a setup for a comeback." (Joel Osteen).

When a person knows you care, it breathes hope back into their spirit. Presently, my son is now clean, following a program that will keep his focus on staying clean & sober day by day. We have to take our burdens to the Lord and leave them there. Don't be in bondage to anything. I will keep standing in the gap, praying for my son. I pray that he renews his mind with the Word of God; it will change his life for the better. God's Word will help him think with faith, and not be in fear, with assurance instead of anxiety, with joy instead of negativity. I trust God will bring him through whatever storms he's facing. I believe God is watching over my son, and he will bless him in a mighty way. God has a way to make miracles out of mistakes. He's so full of mercy. Besides, it is the goodness of God, which leads you to repentance.

"You can have a solid foundation by building your life around the Word of God. By doing so, we would be able to withstand any storms that beat against us. After hearing the Word and not obey or put it into practice is like a foolish man who built his house on sand. Therefore, when the storms come into our lives, we will fall with a "great crash."

(Matt 7:24-27 NIV).

Post-Traumatic Stress Disorder (PTSD)

Most people with post-traumatic stress disorder underwent a traumatic event or experience in their past.

I've met a great person that I dated and lived with for a couple of years, who cared for me, loved me and treated me like a queen. He was an Army sniper, who often told me he never missed a target. He was in top physical shape, a leader and a master in his craft. For some reason, I'm turned on by this skilled sharpshooter's profession, always felt protected, which enhanced my love for him. We had great communication. Trust, no doubt. He made me feel special when he listened and began to pray for me. That's when my soul opened up, and I knew he was the man for me. He had many gifts that I truly treasured. He knew how to spoil a girl.

Later, in our relationship, I witnessed first-hand signs of PTSD. I believe my friend was having flashbacks and nightmares, as he reminisced about being a sniper. He would always have an Army channel on, as he falls asleep. I would have to find the remote, turn the TV off, after being awakened by the sound of rapid gunfire, hand grenade explosion, sounds of Helicopter and Airplanes flying. Certainly, this gave him flashbacks, as a matter of fact; he attacked me twice while sleeping.

One night, he awakens me having his hand over my mouth, telling me in my ear, "Shhh" "Be quiet and don't screen, I'm protecting you from the enemy." I wiggled my body and removed his hand from my mouth. I screamed his name for him to snap out of it, and then he came to himself. He was a little startled over what he had done. He told me he was sorry and went into the backroom and stayed up playing, Wendell B.

Approximately three weeks had gone by before having another episode. It was a very long and busy day. I worked and went to class that night, earning my MBA. I was so tired when I got in, but he surprised me with a bubble bath, candles throughout the house, dinner on the stove, with Luther Vandross music playing. I received a fabulous massage, which made me fall straight asleep.

During the night, I had trouble breathing. I'm awakened by him choking me in my sleep. He had grabbed hold of my gown, choking me, leaving a ring around my neck. He was going to kill the enemy. I wrestled with him, and started screaming his name, he finally snapped out of it, and he came to himself. I was scared to death. I got up crying and went into the other bedroom. He came in there telling me he was so sorry and that he couldn't live with himself had he accidentally killed me. I told him that he was showing signs of PTSD and I'm pretty sure there is help available for you since you are a retired veteran.

Plus, you're entitled to a check due to a work-related illness. We discussed that I was not safe, I should move out, but I didn't want to leave, but we both thought it was best. Oh, and by the way, he sought counseling and is doing fine. Also, compensated for disability due to PTSD. Praise God! Even after all this turmoil, he's still a wonderful man.

Alzheimer's & Dementia

Have you ever watch a loved one deteriorate? Have you ever had to imagine things that are not there? Have your loved one ever say, "I want to go home…I want to go home. I want to go home" over and over again when they're already, home. Have there ever been any misunderstandings in what they saw or heard? Have you ever been upset or frustrated and had to take deep breaths, count to 10, leave out the room so your loved one would not see you crying?

Prior, becoming Wheelchair Diva, I had to do all that while caring for my mother. She would repeat herself or talk about the same thing, over and over again. To keep the peace, I would have to pretend and be in Mama's world. She'll be talking to me as if I were her sister. We'll be laughing and talking about things she enjoyed to keep her happy and calm. Nothing fearful. Sometimes she remembers everything. Then there are times when she can't remember anything.

My mother (Emma), some called her "Tee" became a resident in a long-term care facility. However, before that, Mama lived with me. So, one day after receiving Dialysis, Mama came through the front door stumbling, lost her balance, fell, and broke her right hip. After having surgery, she went to a skilled care facility for rehab. While there, she ended needing 24-hour care due to early signs, and later diagnosed with Alzheimer's and Dementia. Including, End Stage Renal disease, which was the reason for receiving Dialysis 3 days per week.

No matter how tearful our path may be; no matter what kind of adversity you face. We can always find something to thank God for, and we have so many reasons to give Him praise. Some days were good, and some were not; but Mama held on to her faith, which encourages my heart to sing praises and rejoice in an awesome God.

My mother, the peacemaker, met and became friends with four women; Ernestine, Dorothy, Pearl, and Louise. I had the pleasure of meeting all four whom I will never forget. These women were in their late seventies and early eighties, but act as if they were in their sixties, drop dead gorgeous with exquisite taste in clothes, shoes, and jewelry. Although they were beautiful, had men, money and lived lavished, life happened, and as a result, ended up in a Long-Term care facility. Mama was very fond of her new friends; I became to know them and met a few of their family members. She says, "These women are crazy." She goes on to say,

"Girl, I'll be talking about one thing, and they start talking about something else that doesn't make sense." Of course, I laughed.

I met Pearl in the facilities Dining room. Pearl loved to sing. She said, "Singing gives her pure joy every time she sings." She had a beautiful voice. I even heard her say, "She makes love to a man with her voice." She knew how to manipulate a man with her singing and received whatever she wanted from a man. It did not matter if he was gay or straight. She would sing their underwear and socks off. She had that type of power. Men loved her, so she says. She was a beautiful and passionate singer. She had them in the palm of her hands, so she thought.

Then one day, while Pearl was singing, I guess her mind took her back to a nightclub, but she was really in the facilities dining room in a talent show. She saw this woman with a man; she became very much attracted too. Anyways, this man and woman were all over each other, and Pearl felt disrespected, all this was going on in her mind while singing.

Therefore, during intermission, Pearl approached the man and wanted him to introduce her to this woman, and come to find out, that was this man's wife. I assumed she felt like a fool. However, having that illness, she probably didn't. She had it in her mind that was her man. She said, "I'm going to quit manipulating men and settle down with my Boo; in reality, she just met that man.

I met Louise at a Potluck in the facilities Dining room. The facility hosts a Potluck for the residence, friends, and family. Louise was so pretty. She had beautiful silky salt and pepper curly hair. She talked about cooking all the time. Louise loved to cook, and she was great at it. She would tell you that she grew up cooking and baking with her mother and grandmother. People look forward to her cooking.

Louise had no problem getting a husband. She had three long and happy marriages. She could not keep one because they always seem to pass away. Although it was no fault of her own, it was just heartbreaking not having any of them around; as a result, Louise chooses not to remarry anymore. She said, "It takes years to feel comfortable with someone else finding out what they like, and don't like." She just wanted a companion to spend a little time. However, being alone caused loneliness for Louise, which is what a family member told me. She craves human contact, but her state of mind makes it difficult to form connections. I believe she's depressed and needs counseling, but she thinks she needs to go on a weekend getaway and have a one-night stand would make her feel so much better. Of course, we all laugh.

Dorothy and Louise were roommates. Dorothy was so selfish, and she thinks she is better than anybody else is, and she is envious. She makes everything about herself. It's all about me, me, me, all the time. It never fails. She sits on her throne. She needs to take a break from herself. But I was informed that the illness has made her worse. She always wants what somebody else has.

Mama mentioned that sometimes she doesn't like being around her. You can be talking about something then she twists the conversation around to be about her, (does that remind you of anybody). Dorothy seems to think she can have whatever she wants, and nobody is going to stop her. After having a conversation with Dorothy, you are not clear if what she is saying is real or not.

Ernestine is the one friend that appears to be in her right mind. She was very creative. She was my mother's roommate. She was always upbeat and energetic, but Ernestine did not participate in Sunday morning activities because she did not believe in God, and she did not like black people until she met Mama. She called Mama, "My first black friend Emma that told her about the Lord." If you don't know the Lord, never attended church, how can you stop the enemy inside you, from attacking you so that you won't attack anyone else. When you spend time with God, hearts change; transformation takes place; you grow spiritually; causes you to become humble; kind, and compassionate is what happened to Ernestine. She receives Jesus Christ as her personal Lord and Savior.

Often, Ernestine stayed looking cute no matter what. She would wear the prettiest gowns. From the first time I met her, I thought she was a handful. When Mama first introduce us, I said, hello, Ms. Ernestine, and she said, "Hi bitch." Mama told me not to pay her no mind. Ernestine doesn't have it all. Mama says, "She's crazy." Mama was talking loud, as she was telling me this, and I said, "Mama, shhh, she may hear you." Mama said, "Ernestine can't hear well, not at all, you have to holla at her all the time when talking to her.

Nevertheless, Mama did not realize that Ernestine wore a hearing aid. Also, I noticed whenever Ernestine guest would leave the room; she would contact the nurse's aide to sell everything someone would bring her. She said, "When you give, "The help" money, you'll get better service out of them.

Later, Mama's health started declining, and her days started coming close to an end. I witnessed love from all these women. My heart was full of compassion for these women watching their friend Emma, my precious Mama leaving this world to be with my father. Before my mother slept away from here, she yelled for my daddy. She screamed, "Jesse open the door and let me in."

It was just a few days later in February 2014 when Mama reunited with her love after his passing in 2009 and 61 years of marriage. We were blessed to have the best parents in the world. They stuck by my brothers; Pierre; Carlos and me, no matter what. Mama & Daddy, may you both rest in peace. We miss you so much. Thank you for continually watching over us and watching over Demetra; my baby girl in your Heavenly home.

Be Encouraged

Everyone needs encouragement. People crave it. It gives confidence.

Have you ever been let down? Are you disappointed? Have you been through something or going through something that you don't understand, why? You are not alone. Release it. "Let go of the Load" give it God. Don't dwell on it. If you don't, you'll be blaming yourself, blaming others, even blaming God.

When circumstances and difficulties repeatedly replay in your mind, remember your victories from the past will encourage you, and strength begins to rise in your heart. That's what David had to do. He had to face the worst defeat of his life. His city destroyed, their families and possessions had been taken captive, and his men were now against him, but he still managed to encourage himself in the Lord. "David was greatly distressed because the men were talking of stoning him…But David encouraged himself and found strength in the Lord his God." (1 Sam 30:6 NIV).

Friend, I believe I have been blessed and inspired to motivate and encourage you to be all you can be, with your unique self. There is no one else in the world like you. Be okay in who you are. God, our architect, designs us and He didn't make any mistakes. I encourage you to hold on to your faith in God. Develop a grateful heart. You are always giving Him thanks. When you do that, you know God is in control, ordering your steps, and working everything out for your good.

"Whenever God is getting ready to promote you, there will always be an escalation of troubles. When you turn your eyes on the Lord, you begin to focus on His blessings, His favor, His anointing for your life. As you change your focus from your problems to His power, you will find that you have to be grateful to be victorious." (Bishop T.D. Jakes).

Let go of the past. Don't keep looking through the rearview mirror; if you plan to keep moving forward, it will keep you stuck. The rearview mirror is only there to glance back to see where you have been and how far you have come. Keep looking forward to expecting to see the goodness of Jesus. As long as you're holding on to the past, you'll never be able to take hold of the future. Satan will constantly remind you of your past because he wants you to remain stuck in it. But you don't have to. Choose to forget the past. Besides, the Bible states in Philippians 3:13 (NIV), "Forgetting the past and looking forward to what lies ahead."

Whatever you want from others, you become it first. Model what you want, demonstrate affection goodwill, love, and benevolence toward others. When you do, people will bond with you and gravitate towards you, because of it.

Is it peace? Be the peace you seek. Just because somebody hurt you, don't mean you have to stay hurt. When someone is mean or angry with you, hold on to your peace. You be an Eagle and rise above it, even when you feel yourself getting annoyed and frustrated, watch out for the bait. Cease from strife and take the high road. Do your best to be at peace with people, even if they won't take your peace. You move on. Hurt feelings will rob you of God's blessings He has for your life. Nothing is worth losing your peace over. God sees all, and if you do the right thing no matter what is happening, God will fight your battles and will reward you.

"But in that coming day no weapon turned against you will succeed. You will silence every voice raised to accuse you. The servants of the Lord enjoy these benefits; their vindication will come from me. I, the LORD, have spoken!" Isa 54:17 (NLT).

Is it kindness? You express kindness. Be careful with your words; don't be rude and say hurtful things. When we say things that are disrespectful, hurtful or demeaning, we're inviting strife into the relationship. Love stops strife. The Bible tells us that love covers many offenses. Love allows us to forgive. Remind yourself that others are going through things they are not discussing with you. Some wounds are too personal to talk about, they are crying tears you do not see, and feeling isolated in ways, you cannot imagine. Instead of getting upset, walk in love, be patient, and kind to them.

Communicate with respect. Look for ways to walk in peace with the people in your life and put an end to strife. Your acts of kindness can lift spirits and help lift burdens they may be carrying. The Bible says in Ephesians 6:8 (NIV), "Because you know that the Lord will reward everyone for whatever good he does, whether he is slave or free."

Is it affection? Are you more loving? Be unselfish. Love without conditions. Unconditional love loves for no reason. Listen more, get out of yourself, and give your undivided attention. Everyone is talking, and nobody is listening. Blah, Blah, Blah; just talking at each other trying to get your point across. You feel what you're saying is more important than what is said. Try a little tenderness. Humble yourself. When you listen to me, it means that what I say matters. More importantly, I matter to you.

Embrace the way God made you. God uniquely made you the way you are on purpose. Quit trying to be something that you are not. Don't compare yourself to others. You must appreciate, and you should be proud of the path, God made wonderfully for you. So, stop looking at what somebody else got going on because chances are you don't know their story, you only see their glory. You are uniquely designed to run your race. Stay in your lane.

You cannot win what you are unable to face, such as fear of failure. When you attempt something you've never done before, or previously failed at, it's normal to feel afraid. Experiencing failure is the price you must pay to achieve success. You can't get stronger if you not under pressure. In doing the thing you fear to do, that's when your confidence grows.

Also, being fearful keeps us from fulfilling any vision; God may have given us. Step out and take a risk based on faith, trusting God for success. Tough times don't last, tough people, do. Never count God out, no matter how things look. Obey the Lord and don't be surprised when He does what He promises. Just be grateful.

Maybe you do not view the thing that is bothering you as a fear, at all. Whatever it is, and the only way to overcome it is to call it what it is, and confront it. Here's a "fear not" promise found in the book of Isaiah 41:10 (AMP) and it reads, "Do not fear [anything], for I am with you; Do not be afraid, for I am your God. I will strengthen you, be assured I will help you; I will certainly take hold of you with my righteous right hand [a hand of justice, of power, of victory, of salvation].

Could your "it" mean you need to make a change; although change is inevitable and bound to happen, it is one of the most difficult things for people to face. We get comfortable with the familiar instead of growing and moving forward. Let us embrace change and see the blessings God has in store for us.

Could your "it" be you're not motivated to do something; trials and tribulations we face in life zap our motivation. There is no momentum. We lost our "mojo," and we need a little motivational pep talk or encouragement from someone who cares, and that would be me. Don't expect to navigate through life without encountering obstacles. Built into every obstacle is an opportunity. In every question, an answer. In every problem, a solution. However, you look at it; a solution-oriented person looks for ways to solve the problem.

Stop being moved by what you see. "God is not a man that he should lie, nor a son of man, that he should change his mind. Has he said, and will he not do it? Or has he spoken, and will he not fulfill it?" (Num 23:19 ESV) Be a faith walker. We walk by faith, not by sight. (2 Cor 5:7 NIV) Hold on to your faith. "Have faith in God" (Mark 11:22 NIV) Faith takes God at His Word. It's believing and agreeing with the bible. We should never contradict what He says. We should never get into the position where He's saying one thing, and we are saying something else.

Forget about your feelings and have faith in God. Faith is the connector that connects us with the power and blessing of God. All we have to do is believe and speak His Word. One word from God can change everything for you. It can heal you and deliver you from private pain.

Jesus said, "According to your faith let it be done to you" (Matt 9:29 NLT) although the pain is difficult, we must endure. Even though you get tired, persevere. Keep doing His will for your life. The Lord will see you through in the midst of it all.

I've tried Him for myself. Suddenly, I felt His presence all around me. He promised in darkest times in our lives that we would have peace.

Faith does not mature and strengthens without trails. Each trail becomes a stepping-stone to a stronger and deeper faith. As you grow in faith, you will start to "feed off" stuff the enemies throw at you, and as a result, you will become stronger. You strengthen your faith by reading God's Word and praying, recalling God's goodness and reminding yourself that, "Nothing is too hard for the Lord" (Jer 32:17 NIV). Get the Word of God deep down inside you. Speak His promises and receive His power. Then, you have the power to change your situation.

Therefore, when you put the right actions with expectancy, you put your faith to work. You begin to prepare while waiting on God because He is faithful, He is true to His word, and He makes good on His promises. I know my God is well able. He has done it for me in the past. I know he would do it for me now, my future. If you need more encouragement, it can come from reflecting on God's past blessings.

So look back, review, and encourage yourself in the Lord. Let me help you; I remember being at the right place at the right time. While waiting in therapy, there set a messenger, a heavenly angel. She looked at me, reached out, held my hands, and suddenly prayed for me. She encouraged me to stay strong, not to give up. She explained that "God loves me, He hears me when I pray, He sees everything I'm going through, and everything is going to be alright. We must keep hoping, keep believing, and keep on trusting Him."

"You will experience blessings if you obey the Lord your God" (Deut 28 NIV). Blessings are benefits from God. Expect them. Always be obedient and be rewarded.

"No good thing will He withhold from those who walk uprightly." (Ps 84:11 ESV).

Just in case, you need a little bit more encouragement. "No eye has seen, no ear has heard, and no mind has conceived what God has prepared for those who love Him." (1 Cor 2:9NIV).

Just in case, you need convincing of the miracle-working power of Jesus. Here's another example of faith in action. In Mark Chapter 2, I'm reminded of a group of friends, "tear off the roof team" of friends. Their friend had a situation; only Jesus alone could fix. He's in bed, paralyzed. They heard Jesus had come home. So they took him to see Jesus, but when they got there, it was so crowded, with so many people wanting to see Jesus, the door was blocked, and they couldn't get in. It didn't matter; the friends got creative.

Therefore, they took their friend, still in bed, on the rooftop of the house and tore a hole in the roof. Big enough to lower their friend down in the presence of Jesus to be healed. When Jesus saw the boldness of their faith in action, He immediately and publically healed their paralyzed friend. He got up out of that bed and walked. People were all amazed to see the miracle-working power of Jesus. Do you have bold faith? What would you do for a friend?

Friend, I pray that you are encouraged, and just for today, you remember the goodness of Jesus. I pray that my words will lift your spirit, empower you to keep moving forward, because our steps been ordered, by a God who loves us, unconditionally.

Also, we need Him. Don't you love Him? Right now, think about what He has done for you lately. Perhaps, someone you know He's done something for recently. Now, it's time to give Him praise. "Hallelujah" is the highest praise. Can I get an AMEN!

Let's go to Church

Bishop T.D. Jakes asks, "Can you have a heart for something that is not about you?" He went on to say, "Being stubborn has you stuck. Being selfish has you stuck." You are the gift. Your story is your gift. Your history is your destiny. Your success is in your struggle.

You buy what you want and then find yourself out there struggling for what you need. How foolish is that? You cannot correct what you will not confront. We must be strategic and deliberate. Our punches must connect. We must fight strategically for the prizes we long to enjoy. We must invest our energy indirect connections to our goals. No story without a struggle. (Jakes, T.D., 2007, *Reposition Yourself*).

People with strong faith can make you feel "less than" when you compare yourself to them. You feel something is wrong with you because you do not seem to measure up to them. Self-righteous people try to find a way to condemn somebody or judge somebody as if they have done nothing wrong. Stop putting yourself down, thinking that you are humble, by doing so. Also, stop focusing on your flaws and comparing yourself to others. The scripture says, "I am fearfully and wonderfully made" (Ps 139:14 NIV). We are God's masterpiece, and He doesn't make junk.

There is nothing wrong with you. We start as a spiritual infant, and then we start growing up as a spiritual child, then a spiritual teen into a spiritual adult. However, do not stop there. You have to keep on growing because you never arrive. There is always room for growth in the kingdom of God. Every time you read the word of God, you get a fresh perspective. It just gets better and better.

The blessing that belongs to you; no one else can get it because you anointed for your destiny. God has blessings specifically prepared for you. For that reason, do not be jealous of someone else's blessing. We are fighters that get staggered by the punch, the storms of life, those circumstances, issues, problems, or concerns. They may knock us down, but, if you can look up, you can get up. Then somehow, someway, we regain strength and get back up again. We rise from the bottom to the top.

These are the notes I gathered from Bishop T.D. Jakes sermon "These are they" coming out of (Mark 4:18-19)

In an atmosphere that could change your life, you leave the room unchanged. You think, how could you be in that atmosphere, walk out, and not be changed by it at all. "These are they."

Expose to a message that could have turn your entire situation around, but not better by it.

"These are they."

Have you ever been in service with somebody, and it seems like they enjoy the service while it was going on, but when they get back into the car, they went right back to being whom they were before. "These are they."

You come into service to hear the Word, but don't get any effect at all. On the other hand, you receive the Word, and you act as if you didn't; totally unchanged by it. No matter what is pouring in them, stolen out of them. What you don't know it's somewhere between the church door and their car door, the bird comes along and steals the Word, and living as if they have never been sown into or vested in. "These are they."

The Word, your seeds were planted by the wayside. The bird saw an opportunity and stole the seeds. Satan (the bird) is the prince of the air, god of the world that ate your seeds.

"Rocky Place People "

Rocky Place People have no root. Trouble will tell you what you got. When you are steadfast and unmovable, you have root. These people have no root; they will leave when trouble comes. They are there when things are going well, there for the sunshine; not the rain, there for the pleasure; not for the pain. Here for the good times; not for the tough times; they have no root. Trouble will tell all about you; what you made of; there's no root.

Rocky Place People are ruthless people. They'll break your heart. They stay around long enough to make you love them, and then they leave. They have no root. They promise you everything but deliver nothing. They have no root.

Rocky Place People are shallow people. A shallow person receives the word on a superficial level, on an emotional level. They grow for a while, but have no depth, no root, receiving the Word on an emotional level. React, but no permanent change. Whatever you give them, they act emotionally, but the emotions are not a sign of real commitment.

A shallow person can be in love with you, and you, and you too. You here today and tomorrow, over here and over there, react to everything, but no committed to nothing. They change churches in a minute. They change wives in a second. They change jobs a lot too, don't be anywhere very long. Don't marry these kinds of people and don't hire them, either. That's why you have to fill out a resume to see how long you've been there.

Lust & Deceitfulness of riches are the wonder twins of destruction. You make the mistake of worshipping stuff. You worship the gift and not the giver. You pray for the stuff he made and not the creator. They sow good seed, but lust for other things. The thorns and the thistles choked out the seed planted in your life.

Whenever a lustful individual hooks up with a deceitful individual, a deceitful individual will always play on the lust of a lustful individual. Be careful what you wish for you may mess around and get it. You get offered something that's not of you. You drop what is Holy for the defiled.

God will do everything great in your life through seed to keep carnal people from getting it, and to make sure your motives are right. God wants you to have somebody who wants the seed of you, not just your fruit. Don't despise small beginnings. If you are faithful over a few things, He'll make you ruler over many.

Running to You
(Lyrics from my heart)

Can't take it
Can't make it, without you
What do I do?
What shall I do?
Must run to you

"Father, oh Father, I can't handle the situation that has come upon me.
What am I supposed to do?
But, run to you
I have to run to you."

"What else is there to do?
Just don't know what to do
But keep running to you."

Keep running. Don't stop running
Keep running. Can't stop running
Keep running. Won't stop running

"Lord you have the power to step into my situation
And my soul has been anchored
Everything you do is simply marvelous."
"The only thing to do is to keep running towards you. I keep stumbling & falling, but still I

Keep running to you.

"But Jesus, I stopped to look back at my past to fix it. You said to learn from it and let it go.
You taught me how to take my past and find my path."
Keep running. Can't stop, got to keep on running

"Oh, Father, I need some fresh anointing to overcome these difficulties I face.
Even with my unanswered questions, I choose to trust you and run to you".
Keep running. Won't stop, Got to keep on running

"You can make my wrongs right. You can turn my messes into miracles."
Don't stop, Can't stop, and won't stop running. Got to keep on running

"I believe in a God who loves performing the impossible. I'm going to be still and know who you are."
Don't stop, Can't stop, and won't stop running. Got to keep on running

"Jesus, I surrender all of me, as I run to you. Thank you for leading me and guiding me into the palm of your hands."

Don't stop, Can't stop, and won't stop running. Got to keep on running

"Lord, now that I'm in your presence, things are better all around me. I've been purified and strengthened.

"Thank you for working things out for my good and your glory."
Can't stop, and won't stop running
Got to keep on running
Can't stop, and won't stop
Got to keep on running to you

My walk with God

Can you picture yourself walking in step with God holding His hand? Going in the same direction, loving each step you take together. Naturally, giving Him glory, honor, and praise along the way.

The bible says, "God is a friend that sticks closer than a brother" (Prov 18:24 NIV). What an honor and privilege it is to say, "I am a friend of God." Walking with my Lord holding His hand will be like walking with my dearest friend, who I truly adore, cherish, trust, and share my deepest feelings and secrets, too. My confidant, my sweet spot, a place in my heart, only God dwells.

Our greatest concern is getting our needs met, but God's greatest concern is developing our faith. "Without faith, it is impossible to please God" (Heb 11:6 NIV). Do not be full of pride and act all arrogant, as if you got it all together when he already knows; you don't. Humble yourself to the mighty hand of God, or He will do it for you.

Again, be humble. "Do not let your heart be troubled." (John 14:1 NIV) He does not want your heart to be troubled. When you've taken your concerns to the Lord, you can rest assured that the Lord knows what is best for you. "He plans to prosper you and not to harm you, plans to give you hope and a future." (Jer 29:11 NIV). Whatever it is we are going through, we must put our trust in Him. He will never let us down, because He who promised us, is faithful to us. So, since you got a hold of his ear, tell him all about your struggles. He will see you through.

Oh, what a lovely sunny day without any clouds in the sky, air purified, free of contamination as we hold hands and are walking through a paved garden, wide as a 2-lane road, looking and admiring the beautiful greenery and manicured lawns — just another beautiful creation the Lord has made.

Before I do anything, I must respect my Lord and give Him thanks, by saying, "Father, thank You for Your kindness and Your faithfulness. Thank You for always thinking of me and surrounding my soul with Your everlasting love and Your tender mercies. You are the Author and Promoter of peace that will be with me." (2 Cor 13:11 NIV).

"Father, I will not walk around full of pride thinking I got it all together, when You know I don't. I've been holding onto some burdens, that I'm having a hard time letting go of, that You already know and see in my heart. You created me. You know all about me, so I had better be honest."

"Yes, I know You care enough for me, to fight my battles and You'll work out what I can't work out. Lord, life is like a jungle sometimes. In the wilderness; I came across a bunch of weeds and nowhere is safe. With all these things happening all around me, I failed to see your goodness. I tend to lose sight and begin to worry. I needed your hand to guide me down this long hilly and winding rough road to keep me from going under, but I'm still here."

"Father, I made it through, because You saw to it that I would, to prove to me that you would make a way out of no way. Father, I had my share of heartaches, troubles, loneliness, disappointments, and dark days, but I'm "Still Here" (The Williams Brothers).

"Furthermore, I've been talked about and lied on, but through it all, I've made it through, another day's journey, because You kept me and still keeping me near. But, if I'm going, to be honest, I often wondered why. It's been terrifying not knowing if I ever will walk again and be a social butterfly, again. I desperately need to understand what it is You want to do in me and through my life."

"Father, I want to have a forgiven heart. I don't want some unloving action or attitude to stop me from hearing something from You that would save me from trouble. Help me not to worry. Help me to let go of things that are not good for me, only You know what and who is right for me. Keep me from making mistakes. I don't want to miss Your blessings by being unprepared to receive them."

"Give me the strength and power to do all it is You want to do in and through my life. Show me and help me develop those gifts You placed in me, so I can use them to bless and encourage your people and give You glory, honor, and praise. I believe I will see Your goodness in amazing ways. I want the desires in my heart to be what You desire for me. Help me to believe that You can take what I have and multiply it beyond what I can imagine."

"Father, I'm grateful to call you, Father. You're my peace." "Before I was born, Lord, you knew me" (Jer 1:5 NIV). "You destined me for a purpose" (Eph 1:11 NKJV)

"Lord, I'm studying Your Word to understand and receive all the promises You made available to me. I'm asking for Your wisdom and guidance."

"As I continue to seek after and study your word daily, it will illuminate my path both day & night. "Your word is a lamp to my feet and a light to my path" (Ps 119:105 NIV). A light shining in a dark place will shun the obstacles in my way and escapes me from falling into ditches. "But if we walk in the light, as he is in the light, we have fellowship with one another." (1 John 1:7 NIV)

"I cannot hide my light. I'm going to let my little light shine. The light makes me radiate joy. When people see me, they are attracted to that light. Nobody can deny that You have done something special in my life." More to the point, Jesus said, "Let your light shine before men, that they may see your good deeds, and glorify your Father in heaven" (Matt 5:16 NIV).

"Father, Again, I honor You and praise You for Your goodness and for being so faithful. I want to keep doing the right things and not step out from under Your protection."

"More importantly, thank you for restoring health unto me. Thank you for being behind the scene, working things out for my good. I believe I will see Your power in new ways. Lord, I know you got the whole world in your hands, so I don't want to take up too much of your time, but when I'm with you, everything else doesn't even matter. The closer I move toward You, the more my soul opens up, hunger, and thirst for You."

"Father, When tough days come I will look up to the hills to receive help from You. I declare by faith that I've been; redeemed. I am stronger, complete, and whole. Surely, all is well. Thank you for listening to me, and I know for sure You have the very best in mind for me. I love you and will always adore you. Oh Lord, it's been a mighty good day."

Conclusion

Life happens. Every time you turn around, something happens. If it ain't this, it's that. If it ain't that, it's this. There are many hardships. So hard to overcome? How do you keep moving forward? When you have to face drug & alcohol addiction in our own family; When we have to bury your loved one after being shot by a stray bullet while sitting at the kitchen table, eating a piece of cake; When we have to deal with police brutality. They justify shooting an unarmed man saying, "their life threatened" that prompted protests. You know good, and well that your emotions can impact the world around you. Also, when negative leadership made work miserable created a toxic work environment; When a disgruntled employee kills over shabby treatment. Or when Domestic Violence continues because they violated the Emergency Protective Order (EPO). Oh, let us not forget about when children get tired of being bullied. They fight back by killing others at school or committing Suicide. How can you keep moving forward when the humble get killed at a prayer meeting because of racism, hatred, and evil in a man's heart. Or when the innocent are locked up for something they didn't do. However, DNA helped, years later. How can you keep moving forward? When the LGBTQ community has to fight for their rights. They have a voice too. After all of that, there's one thing to know for sure; God is in control. Times up for thinking we have the power to keep people down.

Release the pain you have within. Have that even now faith. Don't be discouraged and give up on God. Get your passion back. Sometimes that's the only time we learn is while we in the struggle, or while we in the wilderness.

Still, the victory I seek is already won, through Christ Jesus. When you have a relationship with God, you will experience peace and receive His goodness, and His favor will come to you. You don't have to live in self-pity. God has not lost His power.

Remember, every good and perfect gift comes from the Lord. He knows what is best for us. If you only believe, you will see the goodness of God. He has us in the palm of His hands. He is in complete control, so don't let what you see affect what you say. God can take what's broken and make it perfect again. God has all power. Nothing can stop Him. He can bring life to a dead situation.

During difficult times, the Lord enables us to see our lives from His viewpoint and regain hope. When I look back to see where God has brought me from, I, have to praise Him. I'm grateful that I made it against all the odds. Just take a minute, look back on a past event, to get a good idea on what God has already done for you. You definitely will be amazed by His faithfulness and His goodness. He always has been and always will be, there for you. Every difficulty we face is an opportunity for God to prove that He is the only One we can always depend on, no matter what.

In Hebrews 13:5 (NIV), God said, "Never will I leave you; never will I forsake you." Have a made up mind to keep believing, keep honoring, keep obeying, keep trusting, and praising God because he is worthy.

You be you, get out there and shine. Don't be wonderful in your own eyes. If you are boastful; Arrogant; Bragging; You are showing off.

Don't let anybody determine who you are; but you, only you decide that. Speak over yourself and your circumstances. Be Humble. Kind. Compassionate. Peaceful. Don't murmur. Don't complain. Grow. Mature. Jump over the hurdles that come in your life. Give Glory and Honor to God. He will see you through. Let's see what great and mighty works our Lord will do, if we just let

Him. Don't be scared. Be willing to learn. By faith walk in your purpose.

All is well, and all shall be well with me because the Lord, our Father, is faithful and He is wonderful. Remember, God is our all in all. He is all we need to get by. He allows certain things in our lives to lead us back to Him. He is in control. Trust in Him and have faith in Him. He knows all things. He is the master creator. Open your mouth and give Him praise. Thank Him for His goodness. Don't complain about anything. Give God thanks in everything. Be satisfied, pleased, and content by putting your mind at ease. And that is having a peace of mind. "Let peace rule in your hearts, and be thankful (Col 3:15NIV).

These benefits come just being thankful:

"Having a thankful life reduces depression. Get promotions at work. Improves your self-esteem and increases your energy; have better sleep quality and have feelings of happiness, and productivity in your life. Being thankful reduces and copes with negative stress; such as envy, anger, and hatred. Being thankful will have you become more likable. Develops a stronger immunity system and decreases blood pressure. Especially if you're taking high blood pressure medications.

"Let all that I am praise the Lord. O Lord my God, you are very great; you are clothed with splendor and majesty." (Ps 104:1 NIV). "We will celebrate and praise you, Lord! You are good to us, and your love never fails, "His love endures forever." (Ps 106:1 NIV). Has He done anything for you? Praise Him and thank God for his goodness. "Taste and see that the Lord is good" (Ps 34:8 NIV). His goodness will multiply in your life. Thank Him while you can. My God is good. Watch and see what He is about to do in your life. That what seems impossible, when God puts His hands on it, will be possible. He is a God of the turnaround."

(Creflo Dollar).

Let go of the Load. Restore your hope & Joy that only comes from God. Joy comes with what you know. If you stay joyful long enough, you will become happy. "The joy of the Lord is my strength." (Neh 8:10 NLT). When we have joy, we have the strength and the power to overcome every obstacle you may be facing. When we think about the Lord's goodness and mercy toward us, you can't help but feel the unspeakable joy that only comes from Him.

Resting and worship is the highest place you can be. The Bible makes it clear that our God is sovereign. He is awesome, and He's in control over everything. We must learn to rest in the sovereignty of our God.

We may not understand why God allows certain struggles in our lives, but we can still put our trust in Him. I ask myself, "What do I believe?" I believe what I know to be and never-ending. Non-stop. Still, it remains the same. Uninterrupted. Steady and dependable. Trustworthy and faithful. Clearly, consistent. That will be the Word of God. "His words are sweeter than honey in my mouth." (Ps 119:103 NIV).

We must treasure the Word of God, and we must respond by obeying and doing what it says. Develop resilience and draw on His power moment by moment. God's Word reveals our motives, exposes our flaws, rebukes our sins, and demands change.

We must get to a place where we're fully persuaded to trust God. He restores hope. Definitely, will experience His peace that's too impossible to describe. Without doubt, have unspeakable joy. Come to Him for protection and find safety with Him.

"May the Lord bless you and keep you; the Lord make his face shine upon you and be gracious to you; the Lord turn his face toward you and give you peace." (Num 6:24-26 NIV).

In Jesus name, Amen!

Thank You, Jesus, for everything you have done and continue to do in my life!

ABOUT THE AUTHOR

Sonja P. Davis is an author, encourager, motivator, lifelong learner, with over 25 years of experience as an Independent Insurance Adjuster has found great purpose during adversity. She penned her journey through her first book "Wheelchair Diva; In It to Win It" to encourage and empower the "mustard-seed" faith of those who may have given up hope. She now chronicles the journey of events relating to people with adversity, pain, and suffering, trauma, violence, sickness, sorrow, addiction, and how faith in God overrides it all.

Sonja reflects her respect, adoration, appreciation, and honor for God while being in a difficult situation people would not recover from. Still, she chooses not to blame God, as we all sometimes tend to do. Nor is she making excuses or looking for an easy way out.

Instead, Sonja is choosing to stand firm throughout adversity with total dependency, faith, and trust in God, no matter how hard or frustrating things get. She reflects a God-given vision to show God's ability to deliver in unwarranted circumstances. She believes her purpose is to be an Answer, a Problem solver. Create change. Renew minds. Encourage and Restore Hope.

Sonja educates readers on "Polymyositis" a rare inflammatory muscle disease that many may see as something meant to take Sonja out. However, as a patient advocate, she aims to bring public awareness about the disease, and through her books; she turns it into a platform to encourage proper medical treatment by using her own medical experiences.

She states, "I want you all to continue to walk with me through this journey, even Jesus wasn't called to do it alone. His disciples were His partners. Certainly, having the "tear off the roof team" obtaining the right people, the right partnerships, are essential for our progress, our growth, and our spiritual development. Push through adversities. Rise above your circumstances. Show determination. Press on. Everything that I have been through in my life has made me the person I am today. Venom, disrespect, and rage cannot be heard. Instead, be resilient and keep moving forward by faith in your lane, while honoring and praising God."

"When you don't tell people the truth; you don't give them what they need to make the necessary corrections" (Iyanla Vanzant).

"God took my scars and used them as stories" (Kirk Franklin).